CARROT
SEEDS

D1070607

A gift for:

_____

From my heart:

_____

# A Hug to Make You Smile

Illustrated by Tina Wenke

COUNTRYMAN ®

Sarah's Garden

# Happiness

was made to be
shared with
a friend.

Time with a friend

is always well spent.

With you I am free
to simply be me
because you
accept what
you see.
Yet you cheer my dreams
whether they seem
silly or stupendous.

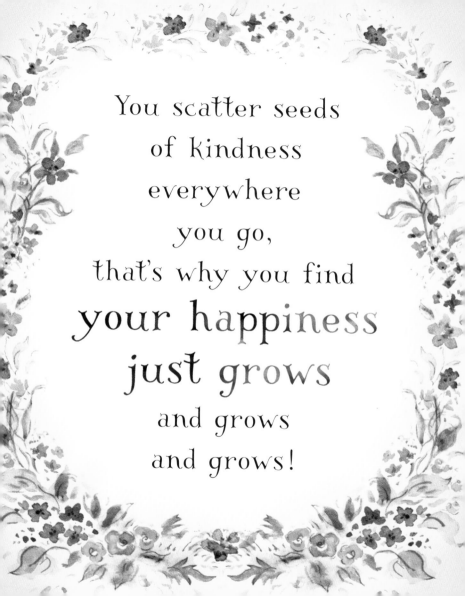

You scatter seeds
of kindness
everywhere
you go,
that's why you find
**your happiness
just grows**
and grows
and grows!

Rain or shine,
friend of mine,
you always stay near
through smiles
or tears.

# Friends love through all kinds of weather.

PROVERBS 17:17, THE MESSAGE

I can always count on you!

Worry weighs us down;
a cheerful word picks us up.

PROVERBS 12:25 THE MESSAGE

Good for you!

You're the best!

I knew you could do it!

Hang in there!

You're so sweet!

Congratulations!

With every page
of life I turn,
again and yet again
I learn,
how glad I am that
**you're a part
of all
I hold dear**
to my heart.

Friendship multiplies
blessings and minimizes
misfortunes.

BALTASER

# A teacup
# is a treasure,
a simple way to find
kindness without measure
in the warm heart
of a friend.

When
I count
**my blessings,**
you are one
of the first.

A sweet friendship refreshes the soul.

PROVERBS 27:10, THE MESSAGE

Cherish friendship
in your breast~
New is good,
but old is best;
Make new friends,
but keep the old;
Those are silver,
these are gold.

JOSEPH PARRY

# A Prayer

Give me a sense
of humor, Lord,
Give me the grace
to see a joke;
To get some happiness
from life,
And pass it on
to other folk.

ANONYMOUS

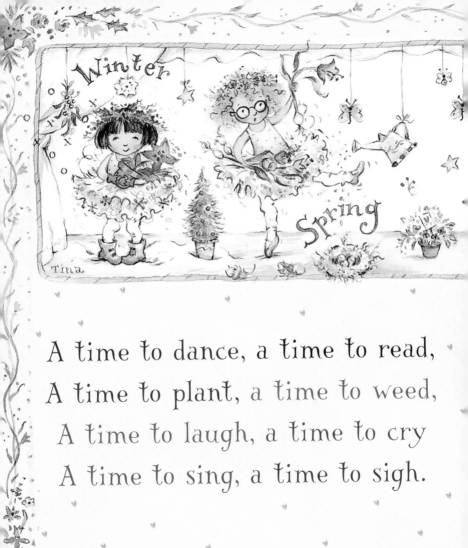

A time to dance, a time to read,
A time to plant, a time to weed,
A time to laugh, a time to cry
A time to sing, a time to sigh.

No matter what each day
may bring,
there's always time
for a friend.

# What a friend like you understands:

- giggles are good

- happiness is the easiest thing to give away

- kindness cannot be measured

- friendships aren't perfect—they're precious

There's no
better way
to start the day
than by saying
**hello**
to a friend.

There's always
room for friends
in the garden of life.

The only thing better
than making a new friend
is keeping an old one.

# In God's heaven
## you're a star...

and how
I thank Him
that you are
such a
**wonderful
friend**
to me.

Life's little
moments
are so much
more fun
when shared
with a friend
like you.

# God Bless You

I seek in prayerful words,
dear friend,
My heart's true wish
to send you,
That you may know that,
far or near,
My loving thoughts
attend you.

I cannot find a truer word,
Nor better to address you;
Nor song, nor poem
have I heard
Is sweeter than
God bless you!

ANONYMOUS

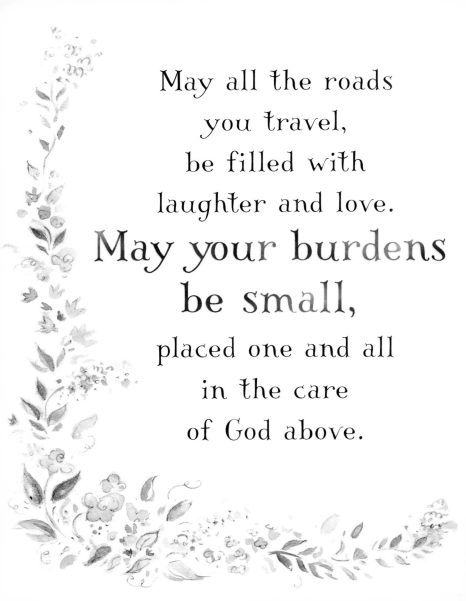

May all the roads
you travel,
be filled with
laughter and love.
May your burdens
be small,
placed one and all
in the care
of God above.

God will teach us His ways,
and we shall walk in His paths.

MICAH 4:2

You have
a wonderful way
of finding in each day
a reason to say~
Hip, hip, hooray!

A smile
shared
is a smile
doubled.

A trouble
shared
means half
the trouble.

The light is **always** shining in the window of your heart.

When I feel blue
I can count on you
to make my gloomy day
a whole lot
brighter.

Friendship is a precious thing.

It grows best with loving care.

If I looked
the wide world over
I would never find
another friend
as nice as you.

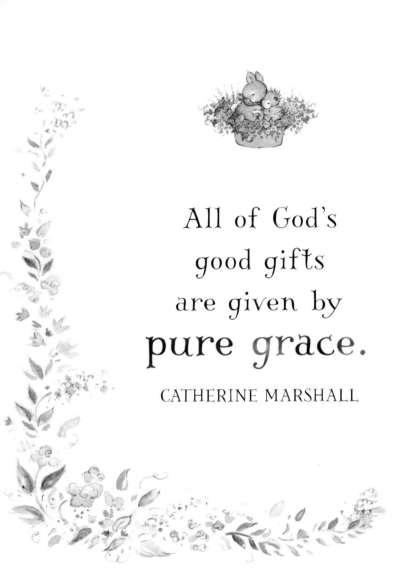

All of God's
good gifts
are given by
**pure grace.**

CATHERINE MARSHALL

A good friend is
**a gift**
from God.

Friends come and friends go,
but a true friend
sticks by you like family.

PROVERBS 18:24, THE MESSAGE

A friend
like you is
true blue.

# When you're
# out on a limb

and need
someone to share
your worries
and your cares,
you can count on me...

I'll always be
your forever
friend.

Friends are like flowers...
each one unique.

Cowslip
(pensive)

Dogwood
(durable)

Daisy
(innocent)

Ranunculus
(radiant with charm)

Crocus
(youthful)

Chrysanthemum
(cheerful)

Rose
(loving)

Laurel
(dignified)

Christmas Rose
(relieves anxiety)

Lady's Slipper
(capricious)

Two are better than one, because they
have a good reward for their labor.

ECCLESIASTES 4:9

Even simple
things are
more fun
when done
with you.

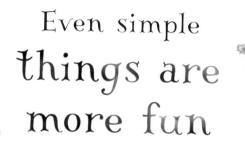

Everyone needs
somebunny
to care!